HUMANITY WOULD BE LOWED THE ARTIST'S YET, BECAME ARTISTS WORD ARTIST, IN ITS EANS TO ME THE ONE N WHAT HE DOES. AUGUSTE RODIN

SOLOMON'S TEMPLE

The European Building-Crafts Legacy

True Men of Progress, COMPAGNONS' HOUSE, LYON, 1993.

True men of progress are those whose point of departure
is a profound respect for the past.

ERNEST RENAN

SOLOMON'S TEMPLE

The European Building-Crafts Legacy

PHOTOGRAPHS BY

LAURA VOLKERDING

EDITED BY JAMES ALINDER · INTRODUCTION BY RICHARD SHIFF

CENTER FOR CREATIVE PHOTOGRAPHY · THE UNIVERSITY OF ARIZONA · TUCSON

Center for Creative Photography
The University of Arizona
Tucson, Arizona 85721

FIRST EDITION

Library of Congress Catalog Card Number 96–84195
ISBN 0–938262–30–0 (Trade Edition)
ISBN 0–938262–31–9 (Limited Edition)

Available through D. A. P., Distributed Art Publishers
636 Broadway, 12th Floor
New York, New York 10012
Tel: 212/473–5119   Fax: 212/673–2887

PRINTED IN THE UNITED STATES OF AMERICA

ACKNOWLEDGEMENTS

I dedicate this book to the memory of Jean Bernard, late president of the
Coubertin Foundation; to all those *Compagnons* who generously opened their
workshops to me; and in loving remembrance of my parents—Frederick, who
taught me craftsmanship, and Ethel, who insisted on quality.

Among the many who helped with this project, I want to single out the following
friends and colleagues for their patient support: Berenice Abbott, Jim and Mary
Alinder, Carla Ash, Fr. James Barrand, David Bolaños, Susan Blatchford, Deborah
Bright, Raphael Campagnari, Stella Cheng, Linda Connor, Rodney and Lesley
Coward, Anita David, Claude Doubinsky, Anne Durand, Michel and Claude Dyens,
Jordana Dym, Albert Elsen, Vicki Ezell, David Featherstone, Yves and Pascale
Gremont, David Harris, Joe Hawley, Leo Holub, Misch and Lore Kohn, Phyllis
Lambert, An My Le, Alain LeBlond, Joel Leivick, Jean Claude Lemagny, Donlyn
Lyndon and Alice Wingwall, Heide Marie, Mac McGinnes, Peter Muhs, Steve Muller,
Terence Pitts, Stephen Powell, Jose Quintana and Pat Soberanis, Jean Renouvel,
Cheryl Seaman, Richard Shiff, Rod Slemmons, and those in the *Compagnons'* houses
in Amiens, Angers, Anjou, Avignon, Cépoy, Chinon, Dijon, Lyon, Marseilles,
Muizon, Nîmes, Paris, Reims, Saumur, Strasbourg, Toulouse, and Tours.

For help in funding my work, thanks go to the John Simon Guggenheim Foundation
for an essential fellowship, the Camargo Foundation for a residency fellowship, and to
the Art Department at Stanford University for summer research grants.

L. V.

Preface

MAKING ART OFTEN INVOLVES a search for kindred spirits, and when Laura Volkerding found the remarkable individuals known as the *Compagnons du Devoir*, the craftsmen devoted primarily to the repair and restoration of the monuments and architectural master-pieces of France, she clearly discovered an enterprise that matched her own passion for beauty, craftsmanship, and light. Having found her kindred spirit in this collective undertaking, which has its roots deep in medieval times, Laura spent a decade making photographs of the *Compagnons'* studios. With a quiet intensity, her work gives us an artist's understanding of the intimate and almost inexpressible relationship between the craftsmen, their tools, and the materials from which they form their art. *Solomon's Temple* extends and amplifies the long tradition of artfully documenting the great historic monuments of France, a tradition that precedes the discovery of photography but was systematically taken up with great ambition and success by photographers during the mid-nineteenth century.

As Richard Shiff points out in his lucid essay on her work, the deep understanding Laura has for the superior skills of the *Compagnons* is per-fectly echoed in the craftsmanship she brings to her own photography. In Laura's exquisitely crafted prints, light is as palpable as the stone, wood, and metal that it illuminates and to which it gives shape and volume. For a photographer who cares as passionately as Laura does about the quality of her prints, and who through them tries to evoke an almost visceral reaction in the viewer, the translation from the richness and subtlety of the photographic print to the inked page is always fraught with special challenges and, not infrequently, with disaster. The devotion and intelli-gence that Laura has put into the crafting of *Solomon's Temple* places her squarely within another strong tradition—that of crafting fine photo-graphic books—which includes such figures as Ansel Adams and Paul Strand. Thus it should come as no surprise to readers of this book and to admirers of Laura's photography to learn that all of her photographs, negatives, and papers will one day come to the Center for Creative Pho-tography. There they will join the archives of Adams and Strand, as well as those of several dozen of the most significant twentieth-century Amer-ican photographers, all of whose works are being preserved to be studied and appreciated by everyone who loves photography.

TERENCE PITTS, *Director*
Center for Creative Photography, University of Arizona, Tucson

Light's Articulation: Solomon's Temple

RICHARD SHIFF

Crafting: Stealth

A VIEWER NEEDS NO SPECIAL information or interest to appreciate Laura Volkerding's photographs. Their format is straightforward, their focus clear. Their composition proves nuanced in ways that extend engaged observation rather than frustrating or limiting it. Unlike much contemporary work in the medium, Volkerding's pictures take little interest in raising questions about levels of reality and photographic manipulation, or in challenging the social and ideological function of the photographic image. Instead they play the role for which the medium was designed, the role assigned to photography since its invention: they document real situations under relatively familiar conditions of observation, encouraging viewers to see whatever is depicted and ignore the underlying presence of the artist-photographer.

Has Volkerding thus attained an innocence or objectivity that escapes her contemporaries who work in other media, or that many other photographers either fail to achieve or never aspire to? Not at all. Like others, she is pursuing a project of her own conception and exploiting artistic resources to execute it. She uses photography as both a device and a language to shape vision and thought, her own and others'. Although she never stages her subjects, she determines their pictorial framing, seeks out particular effects of light and perspective, and knows how to make the scene speak.

To be sure, some of the situations Volkerding chooses to photograph are curious—what is it we are being shown, really? A sculptor's mold, with channels attached and ready for a pouring of molten bronze, is likely to look bizarre even to enthusiasts of metal casting [figure 1]. Viewed at the foundry, the mold assumes a plastic form far more abstract and fanciful than the work in bronze that will emerge from within it. We are seeing sculpture from the inside out. The odd complexity of this form is not the only feature that makes Volkerding's image memorable, for the pictorial effect is enhanced by an expanse of worn and cracked protective sheeting propped behind the mold, perhaps just as much of a visual curiosity. The sheeting enframes the mold and divides the picture into a set of boldly contrasting tones to be played against the foreground figure. Here, the most traditional of pictorial formats—central figure (the mold), with a surrounding ground (the sheeting)—attains a striking tension. A range of tactile associations, perceived through the various visual textures, activates the observer's sensory potential to a surprising degree (and this happens whether or not the viewer projects erotic interest into the sculptural figure). Volkerding's picture elicits feelings of roughness, smoothness, tautness, brittleness, and flexibility all at once.

Without knowing much else about them, a viewer might conclude that Volkerding selects her pictures for their potential as explorations into unusual realms of sensory and kinesthetic experience. There are several instances of relatively familiar objects that have apparently been built to an unfamiliar scale [plates 49, 50] or placed in an incongruous context [plate 52]. And, as if by happenstance, some of the world's most peculiar windows [plates 23, 25] and lighting effects [plates 17, 21, 39] appear in Volkerding's photographs. In each of these cases, a little information about the photographer's locations and the objects' circumstances explains and justifies the man-made curiosities; sometimes a simple caption will be sufficient. But still the viewer's interest in a certain persistent strangeness does not fade. The magic of photography—even in our era of questioning this and every other medium—lies in its enduring capacity to lure strangeness out of any type of environment without appearing unnatural or calling attention to its means of doing so; photography, the most straightforward of media, operates by stealth.

In *Solomon's Temple*, nearly all the pictures are of spaces devoted to the

9

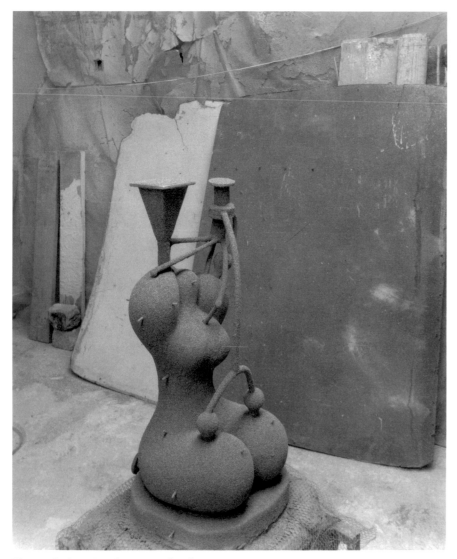

Figure 1. *Coubertin Foundry*, St. Rémy-les-Chevreuse, France, 1985.

a concern she reflects upon and thoroughly internalizes; she applies her own art and her craft of photography to the topic of craft itself. In her technical practice as well as in the pictorial rhetoric established by her finished photographs—from conception through execution and display—no feature is self-consciously stylish or innovative, and Volkerding feels no need to work at distinguishing her photographic art from her photographic craft. Like a cabinetmaker or a stone mason, she would separate neither craft nor art from simple "work" itself. Work, craft, and art all converge for this artist, as perhaps they do for any devoted worker who is fortunate enough to be able to exercise a degree of autonomy. Volkerding's photography has a way of showing that this convergence of art and craft is the rule of culture; it must be so. This is not a new lesson, but one of which a working society should be reminded.

How does Volkerding's photography (call it what you will—art, craft, or work) convey such a message? If it seems pointless to discriminate between her art, craft, and work, there are nevertheless a number of concepts relevant to Volkerding's practice that bear on how her photographs make statements about culture. I will focus on two of them, and on their connections: the photographer's tour and the photograph's time.

Touring: Inheritance

IT GOES WITHOUT SAYING that tourism and cameras are linked by ordinary practice and common association. The camera has so clearly become the emblem of the tourist that it can even serve as a disguise; to make yourself a stranger, an outside observer, simply carry a camera. Accordingly, no one is surprised by a photographer who leaves the studio to travel. As a set of documentary images of various locations, nearly all of them far from Volkerding's home, the photographs that comprise *Solomon's Temple* necessarily address what it means to be a tourist, one who travels to look. They do so in a somewhat surprising way, restoring to the word *tourist* a more precise designation than it usually is given.

To tour is to follow a particular route with a specific purpose in mind, as does a pilgrim who moves from one sacred place to the next. Touring,

practice of a craft—studios, workshops, storage areas, offices, rooms for instruction and exhibition. Except for those among us who have been initiated into the more refined aspects of work in the traditional crafts, the situations in *Solomon's Temple* are likely to look strange indeed. Because the vast majority of us remain uninitiated, we readily become Volkerding's interested audience.

Simply put, Volkerding's photographs are about the making of things, with its implication of circularity, usually entails an eventual return to the point of departure, the tourist having been enriched or enlightened by the experience of a certain set of attractions. With the advent of modern vacation travel, the concept of the tour loses much of this sense of specific design and purpose. Tourists are now apt to believe their aim is recreational, their movements leisurely and only loosely ordered, if structured at all. Any route can be a tour; and the tourist becomes a wanderer, not a pilgrim. The sole responsibilities of the modern tourist are to see whatever sights there are, even haphazardly, and to take interest in whatever turns up on the way.

And the benefit? For more than a century, both common belief and the advice of family doctors have suggested that the stresses endured in a modern industrial society require official periods of relaxation. The forms of enterprise and the divisions of labor under industrialization do not fulfill creative needs or satisfy the worker in the way that activity within a more localized craft economy once did (or so we believe, retrospectively and mythically). Today's worker, fatigued by either boredom or tension, tours historical and cultural monuments believing them to have been constructed by his more fortunate counterparts, those whose work, however demanding or insufficiently rewarded, was forever fulfilling and invigorating to the individual. It now seems that extra effort at everyday work is as likely to be motivated by thoughts of a vacation from work (for which the *extra* will pay), as it is by desire to improve a service or product. This represents an inversion of the traditional hierarchy of work and leisure (as imagined by those who sanctify work). The worker now labors to earn a vacation (a tour) instead of touring in order to inspire a more distinguished product of his own. When workers on holiday encounter famous cultural monuments and assorted curiosities—whether the products of organized wealth and labor or the more modest, intensely personal creations of obsessive eccentrics—their lives are reinvigorated, their tedium and worry relieved, at least for the moment. But under the conditions of modern tourism, it may be difficult to decide whether masterpieces of the traditional crafts actually inspire those who view them or merely distract. Can we still identify with the old ways of working, or have their grandest products become showy curiosities by the roadside, suited only to the passing snapshot? There is a common joke about unimaginative workers who cannot properly attend to their own relaxation—the bus driver who wants to visit a bus museum. Yet we do not laugh at the painter who wants to visit the Louvre. How intimate should a person be with his or her occupation or craft, and how removed? Can work be art? Industrialized society has long been puzzling the matter and muddling through it.

If today's tourist is actually at leisure, he or she at least has the freedom to reflect on the nature of more creative work while on vacation from less creative work. Indeed, this is tourism's most essential intangible benefit: the free time to think and reflect as well as to look. Imagine that you are travelling and are approached by a stranger for information about the very place you are visiting. You are able to reply, without embarrassment, "I don't know, I'm a tourist." This is to experience a certain liberation, a temporary release from duty; for while on tour the good citizen (the one everyone strives to be) occupies no particular place in the social order and feels no obligation to belong or participate. Yet touring is not blind. Advance reputation illuminates and motivates it, the fame of worthy sights having been established by travelogues and picture books. Touring may have become casual recreation, but it is never a chance operation.

In France there is a dedicated type of tourist who visits many of the same historical monuments frequented by meandering tour buses. According to legend, members of this group descend from workers who, in biblical times, travelled from all parts of the ancient world on a tour of duty to apply their skills to the construction of King Solomon's temple. For their modern counterparts, touring is not a release from care but essential to their occupation and their special place in civil society. It might be said that their tour is programmed for creation rather than recreation; that is to say, their travel prepares them for specific kinds of productivity. These worker-travellers belong to an elite society called the *Compagnons du Devoir*; they are apprentices to the building crafts in a lineage of master masons and other members of artisanal guilds, young men and women who commit themselves to the preservation of historical monuments and to the skills and practices that make such noble creations possible.

The *Compagnons du Devoir* aim to remedy life in the industrialized workplace where (in words that echo the language of nineteenth-century social reform) "mechanization suppresses the action of the hand, automation abolishes the role of the mind [and] the individual is entirely alienated from what occupies eight hours of each of his days."[1] The advantages of machine industrialization are speed and standardization of production, both of which can be accomplished by organizing a force of interchangeable workers as opposed to advancing the skills of individuals. Perhaps the general economy benefits, but the demand on the worker becomes stamina rather than experience, a capacity to repeat rather than to progress. For the *compagnon* committed to an individualized and cumulative experience of a highly specialized craft, work is not a time-bound assignment, but a permanent tour of duty and a rewarding art. The word *devoir* can mean both work and duty.

Appropriately enough, each *compagnon du devoir* conducts a *tour de France* to learn from history's most distinguished examples of craft in media such as stone, wood, and metals. (The tour retains a sacred quality not only because of the venerated status of the monuments visited, but also because, before the modern era, the freedom to travel was a privilege granted by divine authority, not a personal right.) The *compagnon* has a special way of looking. When typical tourists view a medieval church facade, they notice only the finished image, a set of sculpted figures set into a composition, a theme for picture books. For them, the stone is fixed in place, its art no longer belonging to a process but to a historical style with a name. When the *compagnon* views the same building—which may have been restored in modern times by the master mason who now instructs the touring apprentice—he or she perceives a living process of quarrying, cutting, and carving.

In 1985, Laura Volkerding travelled to France to photograph at the Coubertin Foundry in St. Rémy-les-Chevreuse, where new editions of Rodin sculptures were being cast by masters of the craft. There she learned of the modern survival of the ancient fellowship of the *Com-*

pagnons du Devoir. She decided to visit some of their workshops, which are located throughout France, and which resemble monastic communities. In effect, she conducted her own *tour de France* between 1986 and 1993. (She writes of her travels in the afterword to this book.) Volkerding's tour, like that of a *compagnon*, is of living work, of the creation and restoration that continue from day to day in the present as in the past. *Solomon's Temple* is a record of her experience.

Volkerding might be identified as a professional traveller—even a professional tourist—who throughout her career has directed the resources of photography toward the study of cultural artifacts. Long before she learned of the *Compagnons du Devoir*, she lived something of their life, including her active engagement with several crafts through the building of her own studios. She has always understood that one can tour one's own neighborhood; a photographer's interest in cultural artifacts need not become a matter of exotica. As I have suggested, one of the salient features of Volkerding's photographic vision is her discovery of the downright peculiar within the local and ordinary. She is intrigued by the fact that photography, the medium that best renders the real, also seems best at discovering the surreal. The strangest images among those in *Solomon's Temple*—the ghostly whiteness of a stonecarver's studio near Vicenza [plate 26], the suspended animation of fiberglass casting molds at Coubertin [plate 47]—derive from the ordinary environments of workers in certain specializations. Volkerding creates pictures that introduce viewers to the open "secrets" of a craft—the odd tools and table surfaces marshalled to bend metal [plates 27, 30] or the household steam iron used to straighten sheets of wood veneer [plate 54]. The viewer experiences a certain uncanny familiarity because work tables, irons, and things that bend and warp are components of everyday life, but the initial disorientation nevertheless lingers. Seeing such photographs makes you feel as if you ought to be touching the objects in question, or attempting the process. There is no other way to resolve the tension between alienation and initiation: looking will not be enough. You want to experience directly (like a *compagnon*?) what each object does, how each material behaves, how each process works.

Through the elements and environments of work, Volkerding's pictures capture the shape of a culture's transient configurations as well as that culture's lasting material residue. When asked, she will say that her real interest is in architecture, architectural decoration, and the building crafts. Put into the context of her photographic practice, however, this definition broadens considerably. Over a long career, her lens has turned toward all things that have been shaped by human hands. For someone with Volkerding's acute awareness of the little patterns of life, every aspect of the built and crafted environment is potentially a concern. Her sense of architecture can include gridded urban pavement or a seawall built of rubble; her sense of decoration can encompass a stencil's precision-cut curves or the casual folds in a pile of hand laundry. This comprehensive sense of design allows her to notice the odd correspondence between elaborate roof constructions and a simple radiator [plate 53].

Volkerding recognizes that all of the skills and practices of the hand form a collective cultural inheritance. The more complicated practices must be communicated from master to apprentice, a task suited to the society of the *Compagnons du Devoir* as well as to other professional organizations, including the universities with which she has been associated, first as a student and then as a teacher. But the most fundamental skills and habits of the hand do not require such formality; they pass from one generation to the next by means of unconscious forms of imitation, perhaps in the way that particularities of speech or of bodily gesture are transmitted without anyone directing the process. Culture operates tacitly and autonomously (and stealthily, like photography); yet the presence of culture can appear suddenly and expansively whenever eye and mind are free to notice it, whenever an individual takes the time to go on tour, recreating himself, looking and thinking, taking stock of things.

Childhood is a tour in advance of official touring and without the need to travel. To the child, new aspects of the given cultural environment appear continually yet unpredictably, each a source of wonder; and the child's "working" response is to look and to handle. For experienced adults, there are still certainly discoveries to be made among the world's artifacts and practices, but rendering them evident may require the dis-

orientation of touring.[2] The proper response remains to look—and then, like a child, to handle things, to test them out and acquire their feel.

The tour is not a nostalgia trip, and there need not be tension between the modern technologies and the traditional ones. In the studio of a Paris woodcarver, a push-button telephone sits beside an array of ornate decorative motifs, some of which derive from ancient sources [plate 6; the telephone is barely visible at extreme right]; a Quebecois woodcarver works in what appears to be a typical North American suburban environment [plate 3]; and the meeting houses of the *Compagnons du Devoir* are decidedly modern [plate 50]. It is simply the case that objects and patterns last long beyond the times of the people who create them through their labor, so that layers of culture keep accumulating and perforce intermingle. The old always inflects the new. Perhaps an essential difference between the experience of child and adult is this: with adult observers, the wonder of age displaces the childhood wonder of novelty. At some point, we all realize how remarkable it is that so much of the past is available to be used and appreciated in the present, how great a collective inheritance civilization offers—not a burden, but a gift. It is as if everything created in and belonging to the past, including its skills, is available free, at least to the passing tourist. It seems only fair, then, to direct touring toward preserving what is already there, and to add one's own contribution, creating something too good to be discarded. Work, *devoir*, is an obligation fulfilled.

Looking: Time

ALTHOUGH WORK OFTEN APPEARS to be in progress or freshly completed at the moments depicted in Volkerding's images of workshops and studios [plates 1, 29, 54], no work is actually shown being done. Only very rarely do workers appear, and then in an incidental way [plates 16, 36]. Volkerding's camera avoids human action and specific personalities, concentrating instead on the evocation of a distinctly human presence with which every person can identify, whether skilled in a craft or not. Viewing Volkerding's photographs, we gain a deepened appreciation of craft and an intensified kinesthetic sense, as if we were the beneficiaries of not only a timeless and inexhaustible surplus of objects, but also the accumulated cunning of many generations of hands. The lesson is that every human hand has its skill. Undoubtedly, Volkerding's own fine craftsmanship as photographer and printer, her cultivated talents and practiced skills, contribute to this experience. But the tactile sense, the sensitivity to one's own hand, also comes about because Volkerding's photographs show the environmental conditions of the hand's application, the conditions of craft—the space, the light, the time. These intangible commodities are as essential to the working process as are the raw materials.

Let me concentrate on the time. Its operation in Volkerding's photographs is multiform, potentially more complicated than the play of space or light, elements that establish a photograph's conventional beauty. In several respects, every photograph seizes its own time and carries that time along with it. Each picture records a specific moment in the existence of its subject, which is also a moment of the photographer's choice. Recent commentaries have made this sense that a photograph belongs to a world of either general or personalized memory the most familiar kind of photographic time. Yet, like other constructed images, every photograph is likely to connote a moment entirely distinct from the lives of both its creator and its subject, a time within a more abstract kind of history. This happens because a photograph has an appearance or style of its own that can be compared with images of its own kind; an image can be made to look as if it belongs to either a more distant or a more recent past than is actually the case. Something as simple as the material condition of the photographic print (as opposed to the look of its image) may be a factor contributing to this effect; if the print is worn, torn, or cracked, it will look old. When the photographer chooses to work in a pictorial style or with equipment or a technological process that suggests a past era (or perhaps even a future one), the image too, to the extent that it reflects these conditions, comes to convey its "time," its present, deceptively.

Still another sense of time derives from the coordination of the mechanical operation of the camera to the movement of its subject. If

Figure 2. *Road Sign*, Kent, England, 1973.

that movement is fast relative to the length of exposure, a blurred image results, connoting the momentary. In certain instances, the blurred image of a machine in operation seems more satisfying than a picture that sets the machine to rest: it is better to represent a propeller at take-off as a blur than to risk suggesting that the engine has either stalled or has never been set in operation. Here we are impressed by a mechanism seemingly faster than the camera's own, which escapes being captured on film; but surely we are equally impressed by a camera that can still the image of the fastest machine—the camera-machine that wins every last contest of machinery.

Let it be agreed that photography conveys time in many different ways. What kind of time, then, resonates in Laura Volkerding's photographs? I will call it the time of looking, as opposed to the time of events and processes, whether mechanical or not. Volkerding's photographs create a stilled time that allows vision and thought to settle in layers and deepen. It is not just the studios and workspaces and objects that retain these layers of human presence, but the photographs themselves, because of the way Volkerding constructs them. They are dense with arrays of things to be seen. They do not record a past or indicate a present that belongs to someone else; instead, they slow a present time for the benefit of viewing. Many of Volkerding's photographs evoke the response that the scene still exists, somewhere.

The character of everyday photography is otherwise. The medium has always been prized for its inherent speed, related to its capacity to capture transient occurrences. With only a little practice, hands unskilled in drawing can use photography to make the most detailed of images; the learning process is quick, and so is photographic production itself. This was the essence of the nineteenth-century revolution photography enacted. On the commercial front especially, the new medium displaced more laborious techniques of drawing, painting, and printmaking. Indeed, most technological improvements over the years have been oriented toward further increasing the speed and ease of handling, so that the skills the Sunday photographer must acquire are conceptual rather than manual. The most difficult thing today is to select and frame the subject through the viewfinder in a pleasing manner; everything else is automatic. Basic instruction in photography—the kind suitable for tourism—becomes a matter of aesthetics, not mechanics.

If popular opinion associates speed and simplicity with photography, it is not only a rapidity of production, but also of consumption. Most photographs require but a brief look, very little of a viewer's time. Indeed, certain types of photographs have always been intended to be seen and absorbed quickly, their full impact coming in an instant. Snapshots—a fast action suited to a fast subject—usually belong to this category, but Volkerding has a way of slowing even snapshots. During the early 1970s, often while travelling, she produced many untitled 35-millimeter pictures that have a snapshot format. One of them displays several orders of speed [figure 2]. Focusing on a roadside sign from her passing automobile, Volkerding incorporated the car's windshield and door frame into the picture as close-up elements. They form internal divisions, some of which echo the triangular shape of the sign. Although snapshots are passing moments, this particular one becomes a conceptual maze, a visual puzzle that takes momentary passing—a complicated temporality—as

its subject. Despite a brief exposure time, the image shows distortion and blur, indications of the camera's movement relative to the sign, the highway, and the landscape. These elements are seen at a distance, as opposed to the windshield and door frame, which are so close to the lens that they too become distorted. The recorded picture thus functions as an index of the speed at which the photographer was moving, geared to the speed of the car; or, it might be better to say that car and landscape are shown to have been pulling at each other, so as to cause each other's distension. At a stroke, Volkerding's photograph translates this vision of incompatible speeds and conflict of forces into conceptual irony. The crux of her image, the cause of her impulse to photograph, is the triangular roadside sign. Its single graphic symbol is an exclamation mark, which is itself pictorially distended by speed. This symbol advises of an unspecified hazard. It warns you to look out and slow down.

The more typical Volkerding photograph, such as those in *Solomon's Temple*, is a slow picture of a slow subject, painstakingly conceived through the use of a large-format field camera—a view camera designed for portability and travel but, like other view cameras, relatively cumbersome. The equipment does not encourage 35-millimeter spontaneity, but rather deliberation and planning. It has the advantage of producing a film negative large enough to render great amounts of detail clearly visible. Volkerding's field camera gathers a comprehensive view. There are observations to be made that could not all have been made at the single moment of photographing. A Volkerding picture may represent a moment now past, but its field of information stretches into a future of interminable viewing. Few of her perspectives in *Solomon's Temple* are panoramic; the field and the stretching are temporal, not spatial.[3] The viewer nearly always feels very close to things, set into the midst of an environment of objects and substances, already too involved to choose not to notice. Like Eugène Atget and other masters who extend an indefinite past into the space of a present time, Volkerding absents her own presence from the scene, leaving the viewer within it, suspended in observation.

During the summer of 1984 and through the following months, Volk-

Figure 3. *Gladding McBean*, Lincoln, California, 1986.

erding photographed the facilities of the California firm of Gladding McBean, fabricators of terra cotta architectural ornament of both old and new design. These images inadvertently prepared her for the world of the *Compagnons du Devoir*, because much of the activity at Gladding McBean involves restoration work and, in consequence, the preservation of an architectural and artisanal heritage linking California to Europe. Another aspect of Gladding McBean's business is the dissemination of existing designs, the reproduction and distribution of proven cultural forms. Volkerding has no qualms about the mass production of standardized elements, which is so fundamental to the building crafts, as long as a craftsman's sensibility guides the process.

Two of her Gladding McBean images are quite similar in expressing abundance and accumulation [figures 3, 4]; they invite the viewer to scan the scene slowly, comparing individual elements among numerous related forms. Both show objects lying in the immediate foreground, as if spilling over into the space of the viewer—a cornucopia, an inheritance.

And both commingle past and present, thickening the passage of time. The first picture [figure 3] is of storage shelving that holds press molds (clay is pressed into them, then shaped, dried, glazed, and fired, to make an "edition" of a terra cotta ornament). Whether this storage area represents the activity of a year or a century is left to the viewer's imagination; the fact that the molds appear to be numbered encourages the sense of accumulation, of inventory, of plenitude.[4]

The second picture [figure 4] shows a space that has evidently become, perhaps by default, a kind of studio-office. There is a simple wooden table, a raised drafting board upon it, a hanging lamp, and, most prominently, a partition wall of vertical planking; tacked to the wall are numerous photographs of casts and of classical sources for architectural and decorative motifs. A few casts and molds hang from the wall or sit on the table, creating a strange play of light to which Volkerding's camera is particularly sensitive. The highlights and shadows that move across these volumetric objects must inevitably be compared with their faint counterparts seen within the tacked photographs; here real shadow encounters pictorial shadow within one and the same pictorial space. Yet this is not the point of Volkerding's photograph; if it were, her project would convert into an exercise in conceptualization having little to do with the theme of craft and the workshop. To think about this subtle play of kinds of shadow is a mental by-product, one of many perceptions that are likely to arise during the prolonged viewing induced by the density of Volkerding's image.[5]

The Gladding McBean wall, which occupies most of Volkerding's pictorial space, becomes a happenstance decorative scheme in itself. Her approach to this wall is frontal, as straightforward as one can imagine.[6] The tacked photographs have been arranged in a grid, but they give a cluttered effect because many of them are torn and most have curled irregularly. The curling in particular calls attention to the material nature of these photographs, the fact that they are of paper and subject to change through time, even if left untouched. The condition of the tacked images inescapably connotes age; the wall records a history of human craft while it displays its own history, the extension of its own use through time. The moment of viewing Volkerding's photograph, extended by the plenitude of elements, corresponds appropriately to the extended history figured by the wall itself. This is a good example of how Volkerding's photography does not depict or create fixed and isolated memories of the past, but rather documents the continuity of an enduring present that can be a source of new experience and ever changing memories.

Did Volkerding choose to photograph the wall because of its intriguing array of images? Perhaps. Plenitude is certainly something that attracts her vision. I think, however, that she responded instinctively (as experienced visual artists do) to the "feel" of the volumetric curling, to the visual movement (really a physical movement, but a very slow one) of the plane of the wall. She felt not only the "real" movement of individual pictures curling but also the "virtual" movement of complementary diagonals created by the ensemble of elements (the most prominent of these diagonals passes from the cast at upper right, down toward the hanging lamp). It is important to Volkerding's aesthetic that such compositional subtleties be found within a visual environment as it exists when she encounters it. Like a craftsman who can sense the precise moment at which a surface has been properly smoothed, turned, or shaped, she makes a quick decision, responding to an opportunity to get a picture that will work, framing the scene in just the right way.

So *Solomon's Temple* is a collection of moments seized, each of which folds into itself paths of vision that extend the dimension of the viewer's present time. The multiplicity of related elements in a given picture [plates 1, 22, 38] becomes a device to slow viewing down to a speed appropriate to work done by hand. Perhaps an even better device to further Volkerding's aesthetic is her use of light to trace and "handle" an array of objects to be seen. Indeed, her sense of the relation of light to materials is unusually well developed. Compare, for example, the various ways she is able to build a picture around light transmitted by sheets of fiberglass or plastic, either thick and rigid (fiberglass baffles used to screen a working area) or thin and pliant (plastic wrap used to contain scraps or dust) [plates 17, 21, 28, 34, 39]. These modern materials become as active in Volkerding's visual art as the traditional materials of wood, stone, and

Figure 4. *Gladding McBean*, Lincoln, California, 1986.

metal. Light articulates every material—old and new.

If touch and the hand are the means of craft, and time is essential to the viewer-tourist, then light is the analogous basis to photography. Light can be the pictorial figuration of an act of touching and a passage or extension of time. One of the most natural of metaphors is to say that light touches. Light enters the field of vision, passes over things as if to

Figure 5. *Stonecarver's Studio*, near Vicenza, Italy, 1988.

Figure 6. *Castroom*, Pietrasanta, Italy, 1988.

touch them, and does so as if to move the viewer with it through space and time. A beam of light is like a pointing and touching finger; ambient light is like a hand passing over a surface. Volkerding's photographic light moves slowly and is *articulate*.

This light animates the Gladding McBean pictures, but can be seen more pointedly in two images that derive from Volkerding's tour of stonecarvers' studios in Italy. The first is from the vicinity of Vicenza [figure 5]. A diagonal streak of illumination, its source unseen, passes across sets of tracings (to be used for transferring designs onto stone) that hang from a wall—it is another example of Volkerding's fascination with plenitude. On the floor of the studio is a clutter of stone elements, parts for architectural balustrades, most of them rounded. As the light "reaches" them, "moving" across a space, it seems to turn those rounded forms by the action of its own "touch." The effect is enhanced by closeness since the photographer has eliminated the usual visual indications of a con-

taining architectural structure or a receding perspective. Volkerding's picture shows no floor or ceiling, no side walls, only objects and the light that moves them ever so slowly.[7] You do not look into a space, but are already within it.

The second image of light shows a storage room for sculptural casts at Pietrasanta [figure 6]. Light strikes the casts from behind; yet, as light will do, it becomes ambient, circulates, and reaches—touches—ever so slowly, every part of the pictured space. This light bestows on the casts the same living volume they receive from a crafting hand. The light moves through space and time. It is appropriate that a second source of light, a second window to the room, can be discerned at the left in what becomes a pictorial recess. The light is natural but has also been crafted architecturally to enter the space at intervals—as an array, a spacing. Like work, this light is both orderly and transcendent. It has been fashioned, but it also creates.

Notes

1. Anne-François Hazzan and Pascal Payen-Appenzeller, "Le Compagnonnage, tradition vivant et novatrice," *Metiers d'art 35* (July 1988): 6. (Author's translation.) The social changes wrought by the modern industrial revolution encouraged speculation on the role that working practices had played in the evolution of civilized human society. For Friedrich Engels, it all came down to the use of the hand, which led to the development of tools and the gradual mastery of nature, and—because of the necessity of social cooperation in the fashioning of the more complex objects—a need to communicate, hence, the development of language. See Frederick Engels, "The Part Played by Labor in the Transition from Ape to Man" (1876), in *The Origin of the Family, Private Property and the State*, ed. Eleanor Burke Leacock (New York: International Publishers, 1972), 251–55. By stressing skills of the hand, the *Compagnons du Devoir* seek to preserve what is historically "human" in human society.

2. Material, artifactual "wealth" can become apparent even in areas of poverty, where resources may be inadequate and disrepair may be the norm, because the prevailing social order must have some basic point of sustenance. The extent of a cultural inheritance is not necessarily coordinated with a standard of living, political stability, or the power and influence of a society relative to its competitors. The element of local social cohesion can be something as fundamental as a street plan, perhaps accented by a landmark structure, a design that imprints itself on a community.

3. Volkerding has, however, a long-standing interest in panoramic pictures. During the 1970s and 1980s, she often used a Widelux camera with a rotating lens, producing sweeping views in an extended horizontal format. Her interest in the panorama is consistent with her more recent use of view cameras and reflects her concern for comprehensive detail.

4. Compare the effect of the numbering on the casts at Pietrasanta [plate 24].

5. Compare Volkerding's view of the cabinetmakers' classroom [plate 55], where the perspective within a large photograph mounted on the wall echoes the pronounced perspective of the room itself.

6. *Solomon's Temple* includes a number of similar studio-office walls, also viewed frontally. Comparing their contents can be amusing—from the classical repertory of Gladding McBean, to the samples of decoration belonging to a Paris woodcarver [plate 6], to the melange of decorative models and family portraiture found with a cabinetmaker on a Greek island [plate 5].

7. Compare the spatial effect of Volkerding's views of work tables and her oddly truncated perspectives into complex working spaces [plates 1, 31, 32, 33].

WOOD

And the cedar of the house within
was carved with knops and open flowers:
all was cedar; there was no stone to be seen.

I KINGS 6:18

PLATE I. *Workshop of a Woodcarver*, PARIS, 1989.

PLATE 2. *A Woodcarver's Workshop*, PARIS, 1989.

PLATE 3. *Le Cagibi*, PORTNEUF, QUEBEC, 1987.

PLATE 4. *Furniture-maker's Shop*, SALAMANCA, 1989.

PLATE 6. *Workshop of a Woodcarver*, PARIS, 1989.

PLATE 7. *Church of the Black Penitents*, AVIGNON, 1993.

PLATE 8. *Woodcarver's Patterns*, RHODOS, 1989.

PLATE 9. *Furniture-maker's Shop*, SAN FRANCISCO, 1990.

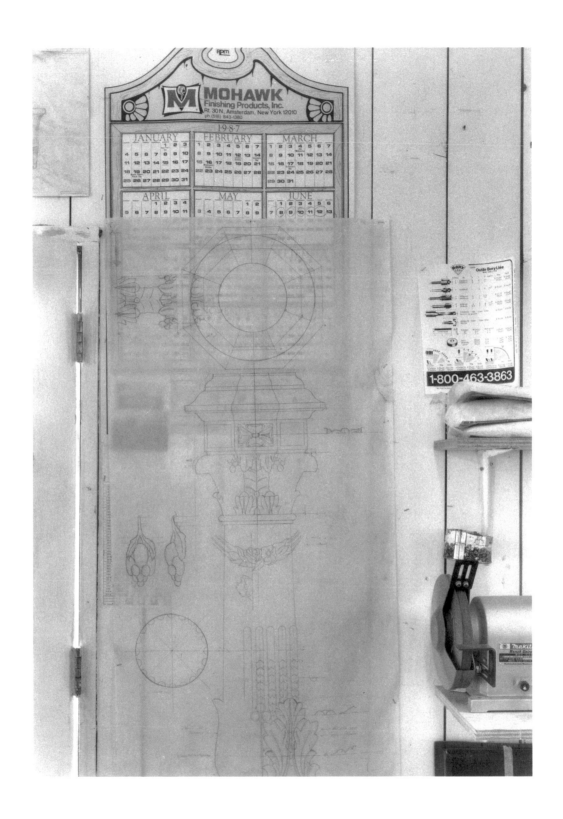

PLATE 10. *Le Cagibi*, PORTNEUF, QUEBEC, 1987.

PLATE II. *Woodworker's Shop*, PALERMO, 1988.

PLATE 12. *Chateau Coubertin*, ST. RÉMY-LES-CHEVREUSE, 1985.

STONE

All of these were of costly stones,
according to the measures of hewed stones, sawed with saws,
within and without, even from the foundation unto the coping.
And all the doors and posts were square with the window;
light was against light in three ranks.

1 KINGS 7:5/9

PLATE 13. *Stonecutter's Workshop*, NEAR TOURS, 1989.

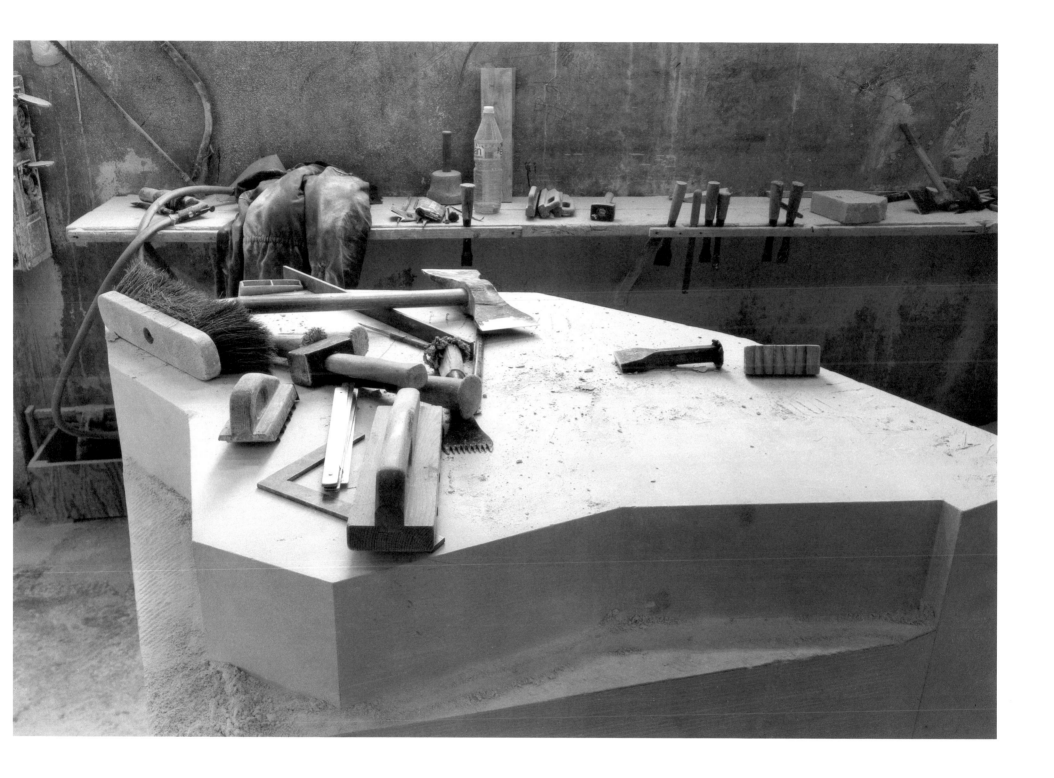

PLATE 14. *Alcala la Real*, SPAIN, 1989.

PLATE 15. *Stonecutter's Shed*, NEAR SAUMUR, 1989.

PLATE 16. *Stonecutter's Work*, ST. PIERRE-DES-CORPS, 1989.

PLATE 17. *Stonecutting Workshop*, NEAR CHINON, 1989.

PLATE 18. *Kings from the Cathedral*, REIMS, 1990.

PLATE 19. *The King and His Cast*, REIMS CATHEDRAL, 1991.

PLATE 20. *Cathedral Fragments*, STRASBOURG, 1991.

PLATE 21. *St. Trophime*, ARLES, 1992.

PLATE 22. *The Eye of David*, PIETRASANTA, 1988.

PLATE 23. *Castroom*, PIETRASANTA, 1988.

PLATE 24. *Dance of the Casts,* PIETRASANTA, 1988.

PLATE 25. *Taller Escuela*, OSUNA PALACE, MADRID, 1990.

PLATE 26. *Stonecarver's Studio,* NEAR VICENZA, 1988.

METAL

Send me now therefore a man cunning
to work in gold and in silver and in brass and in iron
and in purple and crimson and blue.

II CHRONICLES 2:7

PLATE 27. *Atelier St. Jacques*, ST. RÉMY-LES-CHEVREUSE, 1988.

PLATE 28. *Workshop on rue Ditte*, ST. RÉMY-LES-CHEVREUSE, 1986.

PLATE 29. *Atelier St. Jacques*, ST. RÉMY-LES-CHEVREUSE, 1989.

PLATE 30. *Atelier St. Jacques*, ST. RÉMY-LES-CHEVREUSE, 1989.

PLATE 31. *Atelier St. Jacques*, ST. RÉMY-LES-CHEVREUSE, 1994.

PLATE 32. *Atelier St. Jacques*, ST. RÉMY-LES-CHEVREUSE, 1994.

PLATE 33. *Atelier St. Jacques*, ST. RÉMY-LES-CHEVREUSE, 1994.

PLATE 34. *Workshop on rue Ditte*, ST. RÉMY-LES-CHEVREUSE, 1988.

PLATE 35. *Construction of the Great Horse for the Louvre*, ATELIER ST. JACQUES, ST. RÉMY-LES-CHEVREUSE, 1988.

PLATE 36. *Workshop on rue Ditte*, ST. RÉMY-LES-CHEVREUSE, 1989.

PLATE 37. *The Continents*, ST. RÉMY-LES-CHEVREUSE, 1986.

THE SEA OF BRONZE

The goal of the Coubertin Foundation is to transmit its values to the workplace—which
is the environment we expect to dominate life in our present society—by selecting
from within that very environment those committed to the level of perfection
and quality that the architecture and design of the Coubertin estate itself
exemplifies, and by bringing about a meeting of spirit and hand.

JEAN BERNARD

PLATE 38. *Coubertin Foundry*, ST. RÉMY-LES-CHEVREUSE, 1985.

PLATE 39. *The Patineur's Corner*, COUBERTIN FOUNDRY, ST. RÉMY-LES-CHEVREUSE, 1985.

PLATE 40. *Arms of Bronze*, COUBERTIN FOUNDRY, ST. RÉMY-LES-CHEVREUSE, 1985.

PLATE 41. *Coubertin Foundry*, ST. RÉMY-LES-CHEVREUSE, 1986.

PLATE 42. *Coubertin Foundry*, ST. RÉMY-LES-CHEVREUSE, 1986.

PLATE 43. *Coubertin Foundry*, ST. RÉMY-LES-CHEVREUSE, 1985.

PLATE 44. *Coubertin Foundry*, ST. RÉMY-LES-CHEVREUSE, 1985.

PLATE 45. *Coubertin Foundry,* ST. RÉMY-LES-CHEVREUSE, 1985.

PLATE 46. *Coubertin Foundry,* ST. RÉMY-LES-CHEVREUSE, 1985.

PLATE 47. *Rodin Mother-Molds*, COUBERTIN FOUNDRY, ST. RÉMY-LES-CHEVREUSE, 1989.

LES COMPAGNONS DU DEVOIR

The *Compagnonnage* is the oldest of the associations of workers.
The extraordinary rise of architecture in Europe during the Romanesque and
Gothic periods could not have happened without the activities of the *Compagnonnage*.
Since 1945, the worker's association of the *Compagnons du Devoir* has been officially
recognized by the French government, reuniting the various occupations
upon which the *Compagnonnage* was based from its very beginning.
The association has been established in six foreign countries
and has links to every continent.

PLATE 48. *The Compagnons' World*, PARIS, 1989.

PLATE 49. *A Room of Masterpieces*, STRASBOURG, 1991.

PLATE 50. *Maquettes*, NIMES, 1989.

PLATE 51. *Masterpieces*, CÉPOY, 1989.

PLATE 52. *The Chaudronniers' Classroom*, DIJON, 1991.

PLATE 53. *Carpenter's Workshop Classroom*, TOULOUSE, 1989.

PLATE 54. *Workshop for Ebenistes,* MUIZON, 1989.

PLATE 55. *Classroom for Ebenistes,* TOULOUSE, 1989.

PLATE 56. *Plasterer's Workshop Classroom*, STRASBOURG, 1991.

PLATE 57. *The Masterpiece*, MUIZON, 1989.

List of Plates

Afterword

LAURA VOLKERDING

I HAVE ALWAYS HAD A FASCINATION, if not an obsession, with handwork and the skilled crafts that may have had its origins in the basement workshop of my father, a passionate Sunday angler. I watched him melt lead to fabricate his own sinkers in molds carefully hollowed in a two-by-four, helped him gather night crawlers by flashlight, and intently followed the local reports on where fish were running. I learned at a young age that what mattered wasn't so much the destination as the pleasure of the journey, for despite my father's elaborate preparations and ritualized process, he never actually hooked anything that I can remember. His deep satisfaction in working with his hands and his tools, whether he was fishing or refinishing a mantelpiece, has stayed with me. It has insinuated itself into my own values and practice as an artist and eventually led to these photographs. My original intention was not to make a book. Instead, I wanted the work to "knock me around" and lead me to the core of what I was doing. The pleasure of the journey was the driving force, and the photographs included here went through many edits before coming together as a book.

I began working with 4x5 and 8x10 field cameras around 1980, just before joining the faculty at Stanford University. I intended to continue the tradition of California landscape photography, but instead began making views of extractive industries such as lumber and mining in California and Oregon. I found the view camera came with physical and technical constraints that slowed me down and gave me time to enjoy what I was looking at.

It was around this time that I first saw Louis-Emile Durandelle's photographs of the construction of Garnier's Paris Opera, and I immediately felt these were *my* pictures because they were what I had been looking for: images driven by architecture and a specific quality of light.

One hot summer day in 1984, a friend took me to Gladding McBean, an old clay works in the Sierra Nevada foothills specializing in terra cotta architectural ornament. I was captivated by the workshops, which had old master drawings of ceramic ornament curling and crumbling on their walls. It was like Durandelle; I was in love again. Subsequent trips that fall and winter resulted in a series of photographs of drafting, molding, and glazing areas at Gladding McBean. I was allowed to move through the plant at will; I could choose my vantage points freely, and wait for the best light.

While I was working at Gladding McBean, Professor Albert Elsen was overseeing the installation of Rodin's *Gates of Hell* in a new garden at Stanford, and I saw a video of the sculpture's casting at the Coubertin Foundation in St. Rémy-les-Chevreuse. I had to go there. Elsen made that possible in June of 1985; the first of many trips to France began what would become a ten-year project photographing artisanal workshops.

I was invited to Coubertin by Jean Bernard, the president of the foundation. My hosts were Yves and Pascale Grémont—he an architect specializing in historic restorations, she an art historian who ran the little museum at Coubertin. In addition to the foundry, the grounds of the eighteenth-century chateau also contained shops for working with hardwoods, wrought iron, and architectural sheet metal, all joined by paths winding through a kitchen garden, orchards, and woods.

It was here I discovered the *Compagnons du Devoir*; and if the grounds of Coubertin reminded me of a monastery it was fortuitous, because the *Compagnons* have structured their work and life after a monastic model.

The *Compagnons* seemed a living legacy of an ideal of community whose roots lie in the past, when one's chosen work was perceived as a spiritual calling or a mission, rather than a "job." The *Compagnons* took all their meals together, lived in dedicated quarters, and were forbidden to marry until they were initiated as full *Compagnons*. These strictures, as well as the rituals and customs that suffused the preparation for their craft, struck me as an apt illustration of Rodin's statement that work, rather than a means of subsistence, should be an end in itself:

> *How much happier humanity would be, if all*
> *mankind followed the artist's example, or*
> *better yet, became artists themselves. For*
> *the word artist in its widest acceptance means*
> *to me the one who takes pleasure in what he does.*

After two years of apprenticeship, a *Compagnon* embarks on a seven-year *tour de France*, staying at different workshop communities and mastering a craft (stone, woodworking, casting, forging, metalsmithing), in each one under the tutelage of a master artisan. At the end of the tour, the apprentice produces a *chef d'oeuvre*, a virtuoso demonstration of all he has learned that no one sees until its unveiling. If he has successfully completed all the requirements (only one-sixteenth of those who embark complete the full program), he becomes a master in turn. Much of the work undertaken by *Compagnons* involves restoration of historic buildings and monuments, but they are not limited to antiquarian or preservation projects.

In 1986, between semesters at Stanford, aided by the Grémonts and loosely, but not conscientiously, following the model of the *Compagnons' tour de France*, I set off on photographic expeditions to a number of these workshops, accompanied by my friend and former student, An My Le, whose inventory of the *Compagnon's* houses facilitated my travels. Jordana Dym, who is fluent in French, also joined us on some of these trips and served as my voice. During this time I read George Sand's *The Journeyman Joiner* and Gerard de Nerval's *The Legend of Solomon and Queen of the Morning*, two books that left a deep impression, an understanding of where my work had led me. Sand's book solidified my thinking about the structure of my book; the divisions I have used—wood, metal, stone—are derived from Nerval. While these categories function well in presenting my photographs, I must emphasize that the *Compagnons* do not make these same distinctions within their own organization.

In 1987, I received a Guggenheim Fellowship to continue my work on the *Compagnons* and their workshops. This grant, and an arrangement that allowed me to teach at Stanford's campus in Tours, enabled me to spend the 1988–89 academic year in France. Generous letters of introduction allowed me to gain access to the workshops, but perseverance and tenacity were indispensable.

The following anecdote illustrates both the nature of my experiences and my approach to photographing in a country where I did not speak the language and had to build trust among those whose workshops I wanted to visit. While in the Dordogne, I went to the village of Castellones and saw a modest shop which, by the sawdust covering the windows, I recognized as a woodworker's. The owner's grown daughter opened the door and, after examining my letters of introduction, demanded to see my passport as well. "There are many thieves in France now," she explained. "It's not that you're a thief, but we must take every precaution." The shop was small and cluttered, strung with electrical wires, the corners covered with sawdust-laden cobwebs; "*un melangé de vingt-cinq ans*," the owner said. The only natural light came from the glazed front. A ladder led to the loft where the family lived. Only when a trap door swung open and rained trash on me while I was setting up my camera did I become aware of the wife's presence.

Within this twenty- by fifty-foot space, I photographed the cabinetmaker's workbench with his hand tools hanging behind; the table opposite, piled with dusty junk; a broken chair next to it; the planer, with potatoes stored in the shavings below. Wood was stacked behind the planer, and part of an old bicycle hung from a hook in the rear wall. It was crowded, chaotic, and idiosyncratic; its order apparent only to the owner. But it was precisely the kind of space and light that seduced me for its texture, its richness, and the evidence of a life wholly devoted to manual labor.

While teaching at Tours, I went to a stonemasonry shop near Soissons that combined computer-controlled saws with traditional stone-working techniques. I also photographed in Epone, Cépoy, Troyes, and Rennes. At Rennes, I was able to peek at the customs and legends of the *Com-*

pagnons, thanks to Stella Cheng, a mason from San Francisco who was spending a year with them. The graffiti left on monuments by these artisans and their predecessors fascinated me, with tantalizing clues to secrets and rituals, and quotes from ancient sources.

I visited the shop of a *Compagnon* who had just completed his *tour de France* and had settled in Rennes to restore the stonework on the town's Romanesque cathedral and nearby Roman bridge. He shared some of the secret jokes the original masons had left high on the cathedral's walls, invisible to clergy or parishioners. Stone was this man's love; and he told me that at night, in the empty church, he imagined the stone sculptures chatting with each other.

In 1993, I spent six months in Cassis at the Camargo Foundation. Near the end of that stay, Jean Bernard died, and I drove from Cassis to the Basilica at St. Denis for the services. Afterward, Pascale Grémont said, "Now we really are a part of the great family of *Compagnons*." I felt that in the seven previous years I had completed my own *tour de France*.

Today it is fashionable to dismiss manual crafts as inefficient holdovers of a bygone era, useful only to produce luxury for the rich. By the same token, making photographs that treat these subjects with love and respect might be seen as an exercise in nostalgia or a sentimental longing for some imagined lost golden age. Yet I think the lives and work of the *Compagnons du Devoir* have much to teach us about integrity and about the importance of respect for the past. Considering our alienated workforces and our instantly disposable goods, both of these qualities are sorely lacking today.

Mastering one's craft is a life's work; I hope these photographs testify not only to my own apprenticeship to a demanding and immensely rewarding medium, but also to a model of practice wherein pride in one's chosen profession, the production of beautiful and lasting objects, and pleasure in the process of manufacture (MANU = hand; FACERE = make) will be understood as essential to our very survival and humanity. It is in this spirit, as well as to honor the *Compagnons*, that I have made these photographs.

San Francisco, January 1996

Laura Volkerding: A Chronology

1939 Born October 16 in Louisville, Kentucky, to Frederick Volkerding [1907–1957] and Ethel Steinlage Volkerding [1906–1987], and raised there. Life as an only child set the pattern for being solitary and introspective.

1957 Attended the University of Louisville; Professor Robert Doherty gave her an understanding of photography as a means of expression.

1961 After receiving bachelor of fine arts degree from the University of Louisville, entered the master's degree program in graphic design at the Institute of Design, Illinois Institute of Technology. Continued photographing independently.

1964 Received master's degree with printmaking emphasis from the Institute of Design.

1964–1976 Various exhibitions of prints and drawings. Taught printmaking part-time at Evanston Art Center in Evanston, Illinois. Helped organize photography shows at alternative galleries in the Chicago area.

1966 Instructor in printmaking at Rosary College, River Forest, Illinois, until 1970. Married David Bolaños.

1968 Established Lightfall Gallery for photography with Robert Stiegler and Anita David at the Evanston Art Center.

1970 Appointed instructor of printmaking at the Art Department of the University of Chicago. Divorced; no children.

1972 A fire in her Chicago apartment destroyed all of her printmaking work; from then on, she concentrated on photography. Exhibitions include Art Department faculty show, University of Chicago.

1972–1975 Assisted in coordinating a program of photography exhibitions at a space provided by the Second Unitarian Church, Chicago.

1973 Exhibition, *The Edge of Photography*, Lightfall Gallery, Evanston.

1974 Appointed assistant professor of printmaking, Art Department, University of Chicago; began teaching photography there the ensuing year. Obtained Widelux camera to work in panoramic format. Acquired Chicago home and studio. Exhibitions include *Windy-City Open*, Exchange National Bank, Chicago.

1975 Began cross-country travels each summer, taking different routes each time, to photograph landscapes, campgrounds, and motorhomes. Exhibitions include *Photo-Finish*, N.A.M.E. Gallery, Chicago.

1976 Exhibitions include *10x10*, Galesburg Civic Art Center, Illinois.

1977 First one-person exhibition of photographs, *Panoramas*, at Two Illinois Center, Chicago. Other exhibitions include *Panoramic Photographs*, Grey Gallery, New York University; *Chicago Survey*, Illinois Wesleyan University; *Chicago Photographers*, Art Institute of Chicago.

1978 Photographs published in *Court House* (Pare & Lambert, eds., New York: Horizon Press), and included in accompanying traveling exhibition of county courthouse photographs. Traveled to China and photographed there.

1979 Photographed Chicago-area black gospel churches: while intending to photograph the congregations, became more interested in the way the churches looked. Exhibitions include *70s Wide-View*, Ditmar Gallery, Northwestern University, Evanston, Illinois; *Midwestern Photographers*, Kohler Art Center, Sheboygan, Wisconsin; *Artists of the Committee on Art and Design*, Smart Gallery, University of Chicago.

1980 Appointed senior lecturer of photography, Stanford University Department of Art, Palo Alto, California. Purchased a 5x7 Deardorff view camera with special 4x5 reducing back to make multiple-frame panoramas; stopped using 35mm and Widelux cameras; found the multiple-frame technique was conceptually more problematic and therefore more interesting. Exhibitions include *Laura Volkerding: New Photographs* (solo), The Renaissance Society, Chicago; *New Landscapes*, The Friends of Photography, Carmel, California.

1981 Received summer research fellowship from Stanford University; photographed the Pacific Coast. Exhibitions include *Laura Volkerding: Photographs* (solo), Stanford University Museum of Art; *The Panoramic Image*, Hansard Gallery, University of Southampton, England; *Traces*, University of Illinois Museum of Art, Chicago.

1982 Bought a home and built a studio on Bertita Street in San Francisco. Exhibitions include *Photo Art I: Six California Women Photographers*, Photokina, Cologne, Germany; *The Divided Landscape*, Robert Freidus Gallery, New York; *SECA Invitational*, San Francisco Museum of Modern Art; *Critic's Choice*, Eaton-Shoen Gallery, San Francisco.

1983 Exhibitions include *Photographs by Laura Volkerding* (solo), Rice University Media Center, Houston; *Landscape Now*, Fort Mason, San Francisco; *New American Photographs*, California State University, San Bernardino, and Lehigh University, Bethlehem, Pennsylvania.

1984 Ended panoramic photography; felt format was no longer challenging. Bought an 8x10 Deardorff view camera. Visited Gladding-McBean, a terra cotta reproduction and ornament maker in the Sierra foothills: returned there with her new view camera to photograph workshops. Exhibitions include multiple-frame panoramas in *California: The Changing Landscape* (solo), Philippe Bonnafont Gallery, San Francisco; *Stanford Studio Faculty*, Stanford University Museum of Art; *In Perspective*, Palo Alto Cultural Center, California.

1985 Traveled to Paris for six weeks after seeing a film of the casting of Rodin's *Gates of Hell*, which Stanford had commissioned for its Rodin sculpture garden; spent one day each week photographing the Coubertin bronze foundry in nearby St. Rémy-les-Chevreuse. Exhibitions include *Settings: The Civic Center Project*, Giannini Gallery, Bank of America World Headquarters, San Francisco; *Panoramas* (solo), Coos Art Museum, Coos Bay, Oregon.

1986 Spent six weeks in Paris on *Prix de Paris* fellowship awarded by *Cité International des Arts*; returned to the Coubertin Foundry each week to photograph with the 8x10 camera. Read Gerard de Nerval's *The Legend of Solomon and Queen of the Morning* and derived her book title and divisions from it. Exhibitions include *Fourth Annual Juried Photography Exhibition*, Monterey Peninsula Museum of Art, Monterey, California, received first prize; *50th Anniversary Acquisitions*, San Francisco Museum of Modern Art; *The Cabin, The Temple, The Trailer*, Oakland Museum, Oakland, California.

1987 Traveled to Crete and photographed craftsmen's workshops in Rythmnon. Commissioned to photograph the restoration work of the old Shaughnessy House for the Canadian Centre for Architecture in Montreal; side trips to photograph woodworkers and the quarry at St. Marc, Quebec. Exhibitions include *Simple Pleasures: Photography from the Seagram Collection*, New York.

1988 Awarded fellowship from the John Simon Guggenheim Memorial

Foundation to photograph the metal, wood, and stone workshops of the *Compagnons du Devoir*; took leave of absence from Stanford University. Traveled throughout France photographing *Compagnons'* workshops. Also photographed in Sardinia, Sicily, Tunisia, Nice, and Italy. In Italy, spent ten days photographing stonecarvers' workplaces in Pietrasanta. Exhibitions include *Laura Volkerding: Photographs of Workshops* (solo), Stanford University Museum of Art.

1989 Taught at Stanford's Overseas Studies in Tours, France, then photographed in Spain, Paris, and Greece (Athens, Rhodes and Simi) before returning to San Francisco. Printed photographs and worked up first dummy of a book. Returned to France on Guggenheim Fellowship; visited *Compagnons'* houses on list she and friends compiled over several years, photographing their workshops. Exhibitions include *Recents Enrichissements*, Bibliothèque Nationale, Paris.

1990 Photographed restoration training center at San Servelo, in the Venice Lagoon, Italy. Exhibitions include *Laura Volkerding: Photographs* (solo), Concourse Gallery of the San Francisco International Airport.

1991 Visited and photographed *Compagnon* houses throughout France with California stonecutter Stella Cheng. Visited Nash Editions, Manhattan Beach, California; Nash digitizes and makes Iris print from one negative, and she loves result. Took summer digital photography workshop in Camden, Maine. At the end of a three-week trip to France in the fall, everything in her car was stolen, including 200 sheets of 5x7 exposed film. Continued to edit and re-edit the book and show it to friends for response. Exhibitions include *Panorama des Panoramas*, Palais de Tokyo, Paris; Photokina, Cologne, Germany; Turner Krull Gallery, Los Angeles; *Panorama of California*, Oakland Museum, Oakland. Panelist, *Group f.64: 1932 Origins/1992 Inspirations*, Oakland Museum.

1993 April: Retraced route of theft trip of 1992 and photographed restoration of *Mairie* (village hall) at Issy-les-Moulineaux. Exhibitions include *Laura Volkerding: Taking the Side of Things* (solo), Alinder Gallery, Gualala.

1994 Traveled to the south of France for a five-month residency fellowship at Camargo Foundation, Cassis. Began work on a new series of large-format pinhole photographs of the important monuments in the Midi. Just before returning home, purchased *Les Coutureaux*, a small country farmhouse near the Loire River Valley. Resumed teaching at Stanford University in the fall and continued work on the *Compagnons* book. Exhibitions include *The Camargo Camera* (solo), Camargo Foundation, Cassis, France; *La Fondation de Coubertin: ses activites, ses collections*, St. Rémy-les-Chevreuse, France; *Choices*, Oakland Museum; *Traditions Re-defined: Contemporary American Photography*, Wildwood Gallery, Napa.

1995 Malignant brain tumor diagnosed. Summer visit to her Loire Valley farmhouse, which had been restored over the past year. Exhibitions include *The Dream of Poliphile* (solo), Craig Krull Gallery, Santa Monica; *Four Photographers Visit Quebec*, Canadian Centre for Architecture.

1996 Artist's archive is established at the Center for Creative Photography, University of Arizona, which, in her honor, names the scholars' study area of its center for research in the history of photography The Laura Volkerding Reading Room.

Compagnons' Ceremonial Flag, MARSEILLES, 1993.

EDITED BY JAMES ALINDER · PRODUCTION COORDINATED BY DAVID BOLAÑOS · DESIGNED BY CHRISTOPHER STINEHOUR

SET IN ADOBE GARAMOND TYPES AND PRINTED BY THE STINEHOUR PRESS, LUNENBURG, VERMONT

BOUND BY ACME BOOKBINDERY, CHARLESTOWN, MASSACHUSETTS

HOW MUCH HAPPIER
IF ALL MANKIND FO
EXAMPLE, OR BETTE
THEMSELVES. FOR TH
WIDEST ACCEPTANCE,
WHO TAKES PLEASUR